Coming Back

Selected Poems

Dallys-Tom Medali

To the immigrants of the world.

Coming Back

Current Print : 2017

Solara Editions

New York, Paris, Cotonou

ISBN 978-1-947838-04-8

Impression: Etats-Unis

Original Publication: 2014

Smashwords (USA)

ISBN 978-1-310606-72-4

Cover design by Dallys-Tom Medali

For all communications:

Webpage: http://www.dallystom.com/books

Courriel : dallystom@gmail.com

New day

A confuse violence
Trouble the quiet of the night.
Harsh noise and dim light
Kill the shadows and the silence.

All the nocturnal beasts are hiding
Cursing the upcoming solar stings
Man after a healthy sleep
Soon will get up and gather his sheep.

The plough shags the prairie.
The farmer walking on the furrows,
Drink big gulps of dairy,
And with seeds, fills the burrows.

Blind to the snake that girds
Happy warbling birds
Gaily sing a hymn for the Lord
From the depth of their vocal chords,

A brand new day has come.
Let's see what our dreams become.

Twin bullets

Tiny green fingers
Caressing a bruised heart
A heart shattered and bleeding

Two flowers are logged within
One grey and one brown
Of breath-taking beauty

They dived into my heart
As you pressed the trigger
And sent me to hell

Reminiscence

I remember your squared face,
Your lips slowly eaten away,
Your cheek poking mine,
Your hair that I tenderly caress

I remember you whistling, asking for more,
The drunkenness of your whole body
Every night I see you returning,
To haunt me like an everlasting memory.

Here I stand

Here I stand, under the arms of the sea
United with the waves
Going up and coming down.

Here I stand, torn between algae and corals
United with the water
Washing the rocks and wetting the shore.

Here I stand, soaked with salt
With the ticklish effect of tiny crab feet
Pocking my body and licking my skin.

Here I stand, dreaming with interruptions
Looking for a lighthouse
That I may invade and call my house

Here I stand, like whitening
Oblivious to where life is dragging it
Be it the fisherman's net or the cook's knife.

Here I stand, now dead
Tomorrow resurrected
On a foreign beach, ready to roar

Adolescence

His adolescence was a dark storm
Crisscrossed by moments of brilliance
Hurricanes and earthquakes destroyed so much
That there was little left in his emotional garden

There he grew up, in the midst of lust
On a cloud, on a wave, in luxury
Nude strumpets frolicking around him
Yearning, waiting, begging

But he had dreams, hopes, and aspirations
Wanted to feed his skinny soul
So he joined the army like a fool
And died like a hero for his nation.

Adoration

In the temple I come,
To adore the Lord
I come solemnly on this Sunday,
With a pure heart and clean underpants

The day is holy, it's Pentecost.
Trumpets are sounding.
The pillars and walls are richly garnished.
The crowd is uplifted and in the moment.

Together by the altar we stand,
Our hands full of offerings,
Our cassocks white and stainless,
God is alive and his Spirit upon us.

Let's do the rituals as we should.
But let's be mindful of the gospel.
Let's love one another, truly.
Let's help, give and forgive.

Lost and Found

I need a land
One undivided land
To grow and rip
Kisses, not kills

I need some words
To narrate my dream
Bigger than a stampede
Longer than a highway
The dream of freedom

I need a waterfall
To hydrate my deserts
Green, once upon the time
Dry now, and deadly

I need some fresh air, a song
To put my sorrows aside
To relieve my pain
In Soweto and Kigali
The outcry of my people, still doomed

I need some tears
For my old lovers killed by war
Tears for their dreams washed away
O! Mama Africa

Life

The cycle of our days hastily will end.
Aging irreversibly drives us to our death.
We have seen much on the sea of the world.
We have lost to the winds, the vessel of our life.

It is time to enjoy the delights of the land.
Wealth and its fruits are perishable.
Life slips away like a house built on mere sand.
Wrecked castles once seemed unbreakable.

Blessed are the wise and the chaste,
Those who have no folly of riches,
Those who do not envy the princes,
They are content to see them in artworks.

Earthly wars

I hear the lamentations of the koras
And the complaints of the flutes
i see the sorrow of weeping willows
I hear the cacophony of too many cries

Tears of grandmothers, tears hot and salty
Quickly sucked by their dry lips
Moaning of slaughtered children
Cracklings of burned mud houses

I hear the silence of raped women
The tinkering of starved babies' bones
The pain of disemboweled mothers
The pop of brightly colored land mines

I hear the groove of raining bombs
Falling on those who have nothing
I see the eternal struggle
Tearing apart my brothers and sisters

Artistic insanity

Loving mysteries
Wearing perfumes
Greeting the deceased
Leaving the earth

My vase is empty
I crossed the valley
And played the violin
Before finding a breach

I untied your ponytail
We left the lounge
Lengthy hallway
And jumped in a carriage

Those are common dreams
When we get afraid
And our pants are wet
Same old mistakes

I loathe the sea dearly
She scares me seriously
She is heartless and ugly
Let us empty our iron heads

Days of regret

Some days can be miserable,
When laughter vacates our broken hearts,
When stingy darts of pain
Stab us in the face and in the leg.

Some days our quest for self-realization stalls.
The demons return, stronger and deadlier.
Confidence and certitude fade away.
And desire comes raging with an erection.

Some days I miss your presence
It made me a better person
Your lips, so gentle, so sweet
And the wise advice they whispered.

Storm and Loneliness

Thunder growling!
The gods are upset.
Eternal quarrels
Between earth and sky

I starred at the rain
Singing on my roof
Peeing on my walls
Washing the ground

I starred at the lightning
Tearing through the cloud
Heading towards us
Swirling like a fire snake.

I starred at your portrait
Seating in this gloomy room,
Worshiping these blue sheets of paper
Your letters sent from outer space.

Diabolic beauty

Black curvy legs, eyes on fire
She hit the road with her twin babies
Hoisted in each of her arms
Sucking her generous breasts

Big dark metallic eyes
Juicy lips, tomato red
Sophisticated like a rocket
Unbuttoned brown leather jacket.

She is a hell of a woman.
Divinely gracious
Despite her devilish charms
Every artist's dream model

The beach

Sand everywhere, burning sand
Fine sand, tempting sand
Sand appealing but scorching
Sand melting under my feet

Big blue shining under the sunrays
Limitless Ocean touching the horizon
Deep blue water hiding the fishes
Ruthless sea washing the bay

Waves rising and falling
Waves rolling and pushing
Waves dying on the shores
Waves wetting our big toes

Tall and gracious coconut palms
Opening your leaves as if asking alms
Old trees with dried crusts
Your juicy fruits in space you thrust

Topless tanning ladies
Fresh and vulnerable bodies
Bosoms soaked with olive oil
For them I could quit my toil

Kids playing in the sand
Kids chasing other bands
Kids jumping and making a splash
Joyful kids yelling and having a bash

Beware unruly kids
The ocean is a huge ruthless squid
It may lure you to its mist
And unleash its waves in a blitz.

Locked dream

Let's lock ourselves up in melancholy
In the intimacy of warm bedrooms,
Where long dry flowers ornate the tables
Smelling like rustic pieces of antiques.

Your thin braids hang graciously
And your smile could brighten
A city as big as Paris

Whenever you burst of laughter
With your shining snow white teeth,
All my sorrows disappear.

The unwritten poem

I am not a poem.
Don't look me up in books,
Just don't look.
I have no home.

I inhabit a wave, a shiver.
Give me a wink, a whisper.
Pull a face, make a grimace.
Steal a caress.

I came on a vernal equinox.
I came running like an ox
Out of a farm
Will you welcome me?

I have hieroglyphic tattoos
But no claim to fame
Ask the breeze my name,
And whence I hail from

Ask the martins and the swans.
They know the secret.
Quiz them and put it in your proem
Say why I am not a poem.

Daytime sobs

I am foreign in my own house,
Lost under my own roof,
In this poor country,
Broken bikes with flat tires

I am lost on my land.
No mum, no dad, no bro.
No compass, no guidance.
Nobody to help or lend a hand

Life lost its meaning.
Like an old dusty book,
Torn, burnt and ugly,
I wouldn't mind destroying it.

I feel very lonely,
Dragged by habits and routines,
Television and Internet so boring,
My days slipping away

My city backwards
Without purpose, hopeless
The people, lazy and dependent
The promise of change, ruined.

My room pisses me off,
With its grey walls,
Covered with dust,
And the strong odor of swamp

I am foreign on my land,
Lost under my own roof
No progress, no compassion.
Nobody to help and lend a hand

Writing

Before sleeping, I look for a quill
A sheet of paper, square and blank
That I place on a desk
Or next to my bed

When I wake in the morning
Confident and soaking with inspiration
I give the wheel to my emotions
And let them do the driving

Ecstatic and in trance
Like the primordial Word
The one John praised
In the first verse of his book

I chisel my ideas
And carve my rhymes
As they fall and assemble
With beauty and rhythm

At last I lift my foot
And my poem stands up
Strong and energized
Quatrain or prose, it has swag.

Fear

I often hear
From the depth of the dark night
When the wind blows through the trees
Some noise from another world

You may say "Hallucinations!"
But I was really under the impression
Of seeing herds of shadows, flying
Spirits invisible, yet breathing

My hair rose and I shivered
When they seemed to get closer
I ran towards the porch
I screamed and lit a torch

Lo! An army of owls
Birds of the devil
We call them in West Africa
Beautiful yet scary

If minds could be read

If minds could be read,
Boredom wouldn't exist.
People would live together
In harmony and peace

Society would be merry.
Young and old in unity,
Would work hand in hand
Conflicts will be no more.

If you could read my mind,
I wouldn't need to say 'I love you".
And there would be no secret.
Life would be perfect.

There would be no war,
On our mother the planet
All races and creeds living as one,
Would work to make the earth radiant

If you could read my mind,
You would see the dilemma of my life,
You would read deep within,
And perhaps become my wife.

Devotion

In the chapel,
On the marvelous altar,
Inspired by the angels,
I painted mystically,
In a shiny blue robe
With a halo around her head,
A blue-eyed Saint

Every night,
Spirit outright,
The mind clouded with incense,
Singing celestial canticles,
I bow down
And worship her blond hair
With a rejoicing heart

I often say:
Blessed good lady,
My only love now and forever!
She seems sorry for me.
And watch me wandering in her love
Like a blind dove
I should go and get a life.

The porgy

For Marguerite Dumas

Lying on a golden plate,
Here it comes.
A crown on its head,
Carried ceremoniously

Before the feast starts,
In silence and solemnity,
It is introduced to all,
Like a monarch,

Old rusty teeth,
Perspiring foreheads,
The guests tear the deceased fish
On its bed of vegetables

Pinkish and delicious,
The porgy goes steadily
Towards its inevitable end
At the bottom of merry bellies

Dear Sun

A roaster eagerly crowing,
The star soon will rise.
Yellowish ball of fire,
Once again shall brighten our walks.

Sun of my hopes swiftly withered,
Sun of my cries and pains,
Sun of my joys and tears,
I see thee coming, Sun.

You nurture all plants,
And make our hearts beat.
You strengthen the virgin's breasts,
And make running waters glow.

You bring smile to the face of the old,
And remind them the years long gone.
You may wake up the dead,
From the depth of his motherly soil

O ye Sun!
In your garden I will saw my songs
And watch their seeds germinate,
Fiery hymns written for you

Agony

My pale and skinny body
Like a cadaver
On the bed, lay.
Pain inside out

My last gallon of blood,
Loudly beg and cry.
My skin like a geyser,
Burst and burn.

My skull clatters
Like a Cuban drum.
My heart races
Will it stop of exhaustion?

A man in his white lab coat
Comes to me with a basket of pills
He stabs me with a syringe
And I wonder: Is this vodka or glucose?

I will never forget the nurse
With her pink outfit,
Big red juicy lip,
And a deadly smile

She looked so pretty,
When she zipped my bag
Her huge cleavage,
Gave me a last jerk before death

Mirage

A mirage appears and vanishes
Like the scent of the lady passing by
Like the moon at sunrise
Like a hasty squirrel

Mirage!
Like the light of the firefly
Like the ghost in my bathroom

My perpetual quest
My goal forever unreachable
Soon found, soon lost
My purpose in life

Memories gone for good
My days rushing like Ferraris
Mirage!

Odessa

Odessa, place of my birth
Odessa, my city my first love
You witnessed my first blink
As God handed me the gift of breath

I admire the greatness
Of your erudite people
Their hard work and the courage
That made them victors at war

Nurtured by your motherly love,
They make you shine daily.
Ancient soviet pearl,
Unique among your peers

From the height of your castles,
Behold limitless summer greenery
And floating baby icebergs
On the Dniester in winter time

Magnificent gardens of sunflowers
Ornate your heart shaped parks.
Majestic sky forever blue
Twin evergreens French kissing

Odessa, place of my birth
Odessa, my city, my first love
I am a Ukrainian griot
Hailing you from my other hometown

Sleeping on my feet

Before I depart,
Put your foot on my bosom.
Your tiny little foot,
Smaller than a teen's hand.

The veil of the night soon
Will wrap the city
You must leave,
Before my parents return

I enjoyed every instant
Of our long and sweet embrace
Like a tasty ice-cream,
Yet I yearn for more.

Tonight again
I will sleep in your garage
In the middle of the junk
And all the scrap

I shall sleep on my feet
Alone and freezing
But proud and rejoicing
I will sleep like a queen.

Because on the other side of the wall,
You will be lying.
I will enjoy the tic-tac
Of thy euphonious snore

It is your way of expressing love.
Some offer bouquets of roses,
Draw hearts on the beach,
Write love letters and cards.

Some make a loud fart,
Open a box of chocolates,
Steal a hug or a kiss,
Buy a poetry book.

Some stare deeply in the eyes,
That sensual and stubborn glance,
Watery eyes, brown or blue
Others smile widely and loudly.

But you simply snore,
To declare your love
That noise you make,
From the other side of the wall

I will be there.
Still, but dreaming
Waiting for tomorrow,
To jiggle and wiggle

My body shivering,
I will wait like a widow,
Away from my cozy bed,
Away from my antebellum house

I will be standing,
Like a French homeless woman,
In the height of the Paris winter,
Praying and calling on death.

Because tomorrow
You will kill me again
With your kinky weapons,
Those you took from your grandma.

I will be a willing martyr.
You will crucify me
Like our parents back in the days,
It will be amazing.

Reflection

I walked on the moon.
I am a star.
I am therefore I think,
But it's all nothing.

I walked on the sun.
Heat and cold are one.
I am not burning.
Dualities are illusory.

I walked for miles,
Looking for you
Gazing at humans,
Their gestures and words

I walked on the sea
Chasing a dream
Admiring the mermaids
Among algae and corals

I walked under the sea,
Hunting for Medusa,
Counting the wrecks
Behold a star, underwater.

I walked on Mars.
I hate its red rocks,
And frozen vortex,
With aliens roaring

I walked in space,
Looking for your track
Cursing at death
Fearing its embrace

I walked on my shadow
Behind the window
Carrying my cross,
Quizzing my soul

Healing my sores
Hoping for a better tomorrow
I walk towards the morrow
Soon a new dawn

With my two limbs
Every hill shall I climb
With today's sacrifices,
I build my future paradise.

Waking up

Heavy stinky air
Single sunray hitting my eye
Barely opened eyelid kissing the light
Delight! Delight!

My hand crawls to the right
Silk, flesh, curves
My hand pinches and fondles
Gentleness! Gentleness!

A breath, a whisper
Love, sweetness, love
My leg rises heavy and tight
Tightness! Tightness!

My foot lands on the ground
My other foot follows
Stumbles on two things
Chilly! Chilly!

My toes retract
And I scream
Of dread and fear
Surprise! Surprise!

Just some rubber latex
And a red thong
From last night
Memory! Memory!

Australian Samba

Shining silver glow of moonlight
Fresh breeze swirling through the wet leaves
Tall stacked trees fully grown
Long lines of strong little people

Their steps shaking the ground
On the drying floor of the forest
A whistle is blown
The company makes a full circle

Hands clapping
In a thunderous echo
A hell-worthy fire
Angrily burns in their midst

Listen to the crackling
Listen to the roaring air
Listen to the outburst of drums
Listen to the rhythm of heavy steps.

Moved by trance
Women and men quasi naked
Dripping of sweat
Shake their bodies

Hands touching warmly
Waists moving
Whispers, groaning
Rubbing pubis

Let's dance Samba
As if we were in Rio
From Sidney to Melbourne
Let's jump like kangaroos.

The devil's cross

A day under oppression
A night of suffering
A day of injustice
A night gripped by fear

A day of infamy
A night of excess
A day of impudence
A night of atrocities

A day of sham
A night of outrage
A day of sarcasm
A night of sin

Hearts uprooted, hopeless
Broken hearts, in despair
Afflicted hearts, in pain
Wounded hearts, in anguish

A day in desolation
A tormented night
A day of tempest
A wrecked night

The devil's cross

Idler

Once upon the time
Lived a man who sawed rocks
He never had time
Safe to dress like a peacock

Lying in bed through the day
Like a bird in its nest
He smiles to life with jest
As the clock rings midday

A hog runs through the swamp
As a donkey chews grass and romp
A turtle hidden under its shell
Wonders why it is cursed by the spell

A penguin is honing its voice
A worm weaves its silk
A farmer ferments some milk
But the idler only procrastinates.

The dream

I dreamed and saw
Lights shattered like glasses
With my tiny children eyes

I saw a princess up in the sky
Thrice prettier than the moon
Glowing like a chrysanthemum
Myriads of tiny stars

Hordes of birds
Soprano nightingales
Playing a serenade
Pigeons and ducks dancing

I starred at her royal face
Her eyes blue like lapis lazuli
The ponytail of her hair hanging

Suddenly I rose
To grab her hand
But I caught the wind
It was but a dream

Nighthawk

Where can it run?
Away from this world that it shuns
To quiet its torment and cool down
Solitude so beautiful

Where can it run?
What grassy hill or green woods?
Soaked with the tears of spring
Dreaming about nothing

Where to run for a day?
To see the decay
Of rustic cottages
Older than its age

In the depth of darkness
To weep away its sadness
Cursing the rising sun
Where will the nighthawk run?

Tyrant

For Emile Nelligean

At times, you dream of being a conquistador
Lifting his golden scepter
To celebrate victory and power
And finish your opponents like a matador

Like an American condor
You dream of ruling over the sky
And all over its limits, proudly fly
Find the gods and steal their treasures

But your dreams will soon implode
Like candles silently melting
Not even the ruthlessness of your methods
Will prevent your demise from happening

The hearse

Foggy weather, cold winds, rain drops
The sky wore its worst gown
Dark angels waltzing on a late afternoon
How sorrowful to see a casket so small

A tiny casket dragged by four hungry horses
Slowly trotting along the street
Towards the lost ruins of a cemetery
That looks like a lonely cadaver

Sparse onlookers wave
As the bells ring in despair
Swinging harmoniously like one pair
The mum isn't crying. She is brave

Large piles of dry leaves cover the ground
The wind carelessly blows through them
Making all kinds of creepy sounds
I guess death is winning this game.

Love in the jungle

Woman, lay your hands on my face
Your hands gentle like fur.

Look at what is hanging above our heads,
Juicy mangoes, ripe for the palate
They swing like the avocado-shaped breasts
Falling from your chest

Macaws singing, cheetahs roaring
Herds of antelopes in transit
Let them entertain us.
Let them perform for us.

I can hear your heartbeat
African heart pounding
Bloody and red like beets
Red like the head of my boner

Pure vanity

Come and sit next to me
Sit in my fisherman's shack
Life is not joy alone
There are tears too

I gave my memory up to the tiger
I sold my years to the rats
I seek the meaning of my existence
The essence of life

I keep on running and digging
Hunting for dreams and wishes
Everything is vanity
Humans and beasts alike

Life slips away and hides
Behind the beard of a kneeled monk
Sleeping and loudly snoring
After hours of meditation

A sister

For Emile Nelligean

Sometimes I long for a sister, kind and sweet
An angelic sister with a light smile
Sister who will teach me the secret,
The secret prayer of the hopeful

I have that pure desire for a sister
Who will take my hands in hers
To whisper me divine advices
With a melodious voice

If I land on the shores of glory
I will plant for her a garden of lilies
And read this poem written for her.
A sister, a sister

Every day I learn

I learn every day
I learn to live in minority
It comes with a few perks
And many sorrows

Because here skin color matters
And I am black
Because citizenship matters
And I am alien

Negroes are different
Regardless of their achievements
Competencies and talents
There is always a little detail

I learn that I may fail
To get the job that fits me
Like a pair of old sneakers
Even if my grades are better

I learn the civilized jungle
Its peaceful ruthlessness
Its busy-ness
Its lack of compassion

I learn that even among Black brothers
There are differences
Accent matters
So does the height of your jeans

You are Black
But I don't know you
Everyone in his own corner
Live on his toes

As a Christian, I hang in tight
Blessing those who cursed me
Loving those who hate
Hugging those who bite

I endure it all sweeter than ever
Overcoming adversity
Believing, praying, hoping
I learn monotony

Same wide room
Same white house
Same laptop, best friend
Same classmates and girlfriends

I learn to survive
Trusting in God
Rising tide of expenses
No income whatsoever

But I keep on living, of hope
Belief that I may pass
Even without textbooks
Despite the parties and the trips

Nobody but God
Nobody but myself
And memories of relatives
To carry me through

Relatives hundred miles away
In Africa and in Europe
I learn survival
I learn a new life

Black

Black is my name. Black is my race.
Thank you Lord for making me black,
A bundle of all the pains in the world

I am grateful for the shape of my skull,
Made to carry the earth
I am not afraid.

I am proud of the shape of my nose.
Wide enough to smell the fragrances
Of sacrifice, hard work and dedication

I am hospitable, even for my enemies
Those who build walls,
Those who sink boats

Black is my name. Black is my race.
I am proud of all my features,
Proud to feed the world with my gems and grains

Hymn to the peasants

Work the soil with your tools
Work farmer work
Because you won't be fed
If you just sit around

Work the land of your fathers
Work farmer work
Humans can forsake
But the earth won't lie

The cattle can die.
Gods may not respond.
But the earth won't lie
It won't let you starve

She fed your mothers
She will keep you warm
Pray the sky for water
And green grass

For colorful fruits
And generous crops
Work farmer work
Work the soil with your tools

Nature is trustworthy
The earth won't lie
Work farmer work
Work while it is still time

Awakening call

Trees are burning in the bush. Ging Ko
Smoke and smog on our cities Ging Ko
Rumbling and rising waters. Ging Ko
A party for vultures and gators Ging Ko

Rotting bodies, fat and skinny Ging Ko
Death waltzing to the music of gunfire Ging Ko
Burning bread, burning farm Ging Ko
Crying widow, crying orphan Ging Ko

Flowing blood, flooding rivers Ging Ko
Nightmares days and nights Ging Ko
Death is very pleased. Ging Ko
He runs out of desires to satisfy. Ging Ko

The butcher is exhilarated. Ging Ko
The tyrant is entertained. Ging Ko
Bullets are flying, fire is raining. Ging Ko
The devil is celebrating. Ging Ko

Brainless mindless

A paper snake flies towards me
Crushes me and steals my mouth
The wind lifts me
I lost my brain

Barely illuminated station
Impatient and rushing legs
I await the train of my mind
Like winter expects spring

O night, thou felt over. It's dark.
I listen as the frogs croak and bark
Their ear-piercing serenade
Glide under my bed sheet

I carry a knife and a flag
I am mad and it is sad
Memories, old comrades
I expect you around the corner

When fire again unite us
For our fairytales reading sessions
With thirsty vampires and lovely elves
Ghosts still hunting my imagination

Pain

An unforeseen dart
Shattered his heart
Pitiful avenger of an unjust row
Now, sad victim of an unfair blow

He stands still and his broken soul
Gives up to the punch that kills
His frozen mind knows all is finished
But wonder why he was punished.

Cruel fate for a man so good,
To perish like a thug in the hood

Banana fields

Acres of tropical greenery
Supple trunks spurting
From the black compost heap
Intertwined banana trees

Wide foliage swinging
Like paper sheets
Waving like a star-spangled banner
Like young ballerinas practicing.

Standing straight and proud
With their heavy backpacks
A bunch of bananas hard like glans,
Soon will be ripe and good

Mbalax

The drum is crackling again.
Stretched leather on an acacia bowl
So dry it creates a rhythm.

Nimble teenagers
Listen to the sound
And answer in Wolof.

You dance it by opening your legs
Bending up and down,
Swinging your knees

It is so fast and jerky.
Now stop.
Now move your waist.

The wind like a voyeur
Lifts the colorful loincloths
And peeps under

Hands open, legs open.
Bellies turning
Acrobatics, high jumps.

The music makes you fly
And can get you high,
But there is no bush to be seen.

Musically yours

May the gentle touch of your fingers
One more time caress this guitar
Masturbate its tiny strings with your cigar
And treat them not like strangers

A magnificent glittering chandelier
Shine some light on a lonely Picasso
A copy of L'anis del mono
Fancy decor and jugs of beer

Play for me with bravado
Lift me to the sky
Amaze me, don't be shy
I want to waltz and tango

I want to swing till dawn
Till I crumble under the toll
And sweat off all the ethanol
Till your last yawn

May the overpowering grip of your lips
Hold onto the clarinet by its tip
And blow it like a black cock
Play until we all choke.

My isle under the wind

My isle is under the wind.
The waves are feisty.
It may rain indeed.

Sweet whisper of the breeze
Singing the upcoming spring
I lay on a bed on the beach
A sand bed, wet and dirty

Solitude is my way of life
I am hoping to die in it.
Alone on my lost isle
I feel happy and jolly

With my Pharrell's hat on
And these torn fisherman pants
As my only riches

Square moon

The moon is round
Melting the wax of all our illusions
Like mirages and shadows
When we cross into the other world

The moon is a crescent
With powerful scents of incense,
Dancing among the stars

The moon is square
Covered with sterling silver
And other exotic jewelries

Be my moon someday
Be my moon today
Be my moon forever.

Listen to the sea

Quiet folks! The sea is talking.
She is talking about giant fishes
Feeding on tongues, genitals and brains

Humans dumped in the water
Humans tripped over
Humans murdered for fun
Humans embalmed with saliva

Women and children
Tiny boats jam-packed
The strongest healthiest Negroes
Those unable to swim

The sea is revealing the names
She talks about drowned bodies
About bloody sunsets
And deleterious walks

She even knows the slave traders
She remember the taste of their pee
And bear witness for their deeds
The sea is talking.

Tell me why

Why does shame fit us like a bespoke suit?
Truckloads of lies
Repeated daily by the voices in our heads

Why are we still bending and bowing
To the plight of dictators and murderers
The buddies of the former colons

Why come to life, grow and die
So fast, so young, leaving no imprint,
Anonymous, irrelevant, unknown

Why carry on hopelessly
In the comfort of poverty
Instead of changing, thriving

Why wait for providence
Begging, asking for alms
With those healthy palms

Why be a puppet blown by the wind
Carried right and left by wolves
Manipulated by the Useless Network

Why not burn the weapons
Rise united and rebuild our broken continent
For twenty seven years I could not find why.

Girls weeping

Groaning, distress
African girls screaming
Young, school dropouts
Abducted from moms' arms

In search for an illusory El Dorado
Shipped to a destination unknown
Smuggled, carried like luggage
To a modern concentration camp

Drowned anonymously on remote coasts
Bound by the chains of pimps
And amoral accomplices
Rapes, STDs, fatherless pregnancies

Groan again and moan
Miserable, hopeless, helpless
Little, loss, innocent
African girls screaming

The needy

Flocks of paupers
Walking corpses
Skeletons like on TV
But the country is at peace

Misery, hunger, thirst
Old flat bellies
God blaming, cursing
Bareness, destitution

Flocks of beggars
Pampered with rags
Cadging for bread
Grass, worms, anything edible

The dedication they lack in school
They show at church
And in line at the shoes stores
Posthumous salvation

Chief laziness officer
Senior gossip engineer
Hard to reason when one starves
Blind to ones infinite potential

The country is sick

Bad roads
Toxic smoke
Throng of used cars and cheap motorbikes
World War I trucks and trains

Aquatic men, friends of the frogs
Industrial farms of mosquitoes
Expired cans, fake pills
Corruption based governance

Mediocrity as an official religion
Unenforced laws, Impunity
Illiterate graduates
Triple digit unemployment

Stupid intellectuals
Decorated embezzlers
Buzzwords' democracy
Useless conferences

Head turning economic policies
Looted public companies
A country sick and agonizing
Forsaken by its people

Sorrows of life

Flow! We are flowing.
All is shallow.
We all will die.
The daily grind continues.
Life like an old castle,
Slowly crumbles.
Days come.
Days go.
Flying like darts.
Death is lurking,
Slowly robbing us of our life.
What is stealing our days?
The devils? No.
They bloom in the sands
And in our imagination
The gods? No.
They burn
In the fires we nurture
Work? No.
Work made us
And still feed us
Love? No.
Most of us lost it already
Money? Maybe
So few of us understand it anyway
Routine? Maybe
She easily blinds us
And binds us
Ignorance? Likely
It is the worst of all evils.
But so few even know that

Food and flowers

Tiny well-kept garden
Bustling cornflowers and roses
Joyful yellow butterflies
Jumping from leaves to buds

Melancholic ambiance
Vibrant colors
Exotic decors

Across the kitchen window,
Francine is roasting veggies
And melting French smelly cheeses

She will fix lunch
And give us something to munch.
I love some sweet apple pie,
And for ice cream can die.

Ode to the hand

My hand will roll on the plains of your body,
Caressing your curves and your flesh
Your muscles will respond by bracing,
As you whistle and beg for more.

On every inch of your skin
Moist soft and sweet skin
Rubbed with coconut oil
My hand will go faster and lower.

My hand will dive deeper,
And pull you in a jug of delights.
You will be jolted and vibrate like a harp
Played by a virtuoso

Stretched, wide opened,
Like a book, an old bible,
My hand will turn your pages,
And keep them safe.

I want a baby

I soaked my body with vanilla extract.
I had it massaged eight days in a row,
To ensure its fragrance bedazzles you.

I gave extra care to my nipples.
Little pink tits,
You won't stop biting and licking.

On my black king size bed,
Or on my red game-of-thrones couch,
Come, lay and cum.

Come and drink my liquor.
Drink from my fountain.
Taste at least some milk.

For you, I will sing and bebop.
For you, I will also twerk
To keep you awake and erect

I will do anything you want.
Even the craziest and dumbest
I will scratch your back if needed.

But you will keep your promise.
You will be strong and long.
You will give me that first baby.

Death is no more

Let's wipe our tears.
Let's all calm down.
Death is no more.
It had a heart attack.

Death is dead.
Cry no more.
Sob no more.
Howl no more.

We somehow made it.
We are the chosen ones.
The humble, the few, the godly
The artisans of perfection

Now, which is the scariest?
To die or to live?
Go, learn, eat, play, laugh, cry, and work
Dream, help, fuck, pray and come back.

Butterfly

Listen to the voice of the Donna.
The beautiful lady calling you
Calling you from behind the lilies
The blowing paradise lilies

You will see the fall leaves dry.
Winter will bury the land.
Spring will bring mommy back.
But the summer sun will kiss your bikini.

Your hard work will pay off.
So much time spent crawling over leaves and rocks.
Your pupa wings will finally deploy.
And you will fly mightily.

Listen to the voice of the Donna.
The beautiful lady calling you
Calling you from behind the lilies
The lilies, the butterfly's prime playground.

The thinker's hymn

This is for you, my homonym.
Master writer of many rhymes
Whether you live in Beijing or Nimes
Your poems have the freshness of the thyme.

This is for you, philosophe.
Lover of allegories and metaphors
Baker of long stanzas and tiny haikus
Wiseman, strongman

Your mighty quill
Delights and enthralls us.
You make our lives better,
And our minds nimbler

This is for you, thinker.
Our guardian, our savior
You keep our saw sharp
And our heart mellow.

Everything has a soul

Everything has a soul
A pure albeit invisible essence
An energy at the core,
That nobody suspects.

Everything has some usefulness
A role to play
A need to fulfill
In our daily human lives

Everything needs some love.
To be desired and cared about.
To be relevant and helpful,
Rather than futile and dusty

Everything is ephemeral,
Just like its owner.
Everything has a soul
That follows its shadow.

Everything has a soul
A pure albeit invisible essence
An energy at the core,
That nobody suspects.

Unruly child

There was in the parking lot,
Abandoned since a few years,
A big sedan, white like an old tooth
But motionless like the statues in Bryant Park

The car ruled over the courtyard,
Like a huge junk of plaster.
Some days, the youngest kid of the house
Would jump through the window and take a drive.

He would wait until his dad departs
Before starting his shenanigans
He would open the drawer
Grab the keys and go for a simulated ride.

Unruly and carefree,
He didn't fear a thing.
To anyone who might give him away,
He offered the promise of retaliation.

The broken violin

As the golden bow was scratching it,
The violin broke down, torn by sadness.
Earlier tonight, darling
When you were playing Pavarotti

I was so merry, watching you.
My love was big, my boner was bigger.
Toggling between the melody and your bosom
I felt like the violin itself.

From now on, and forever
The instrument will rest in a case,
A sleek and glossy sarcophagus
That will hide it for prosperity.

One less Stradivarius,
One more broken heart
The violin is dead,
But the dream is alive.

Giving you my rhymes

I am giving you these rhymes for the ages.
Please hold on to them.
The great, the good and the lame

I am giving you these rhymes for the ages.
If my name somehow manage
To survive the waves of time,

I am giving you these rhymes for the ages.
They may inspire someone.
They may someday be worth a dime.

I am giving you these rhymes for the ages.
Since dawn, you were destined to be the one,
To hold my hand and make me better.

I am giving you these rhymes for the ages.
What can my dry lips now say?
How can I repay your devotion?

I am giving you these rhymes for the ages.
Call this a poem
Or call it a letter.

I am giving you these rhymes for the ages.
I wrote them with your portrait on my lap.
Now I go, I dive for my last nap.

List of Poems

Thank you for reading my book! If you were moved, please take a moment to leave me a review on your favorite retailer's website and feel free to reach out with any question or comment.
Thanks!
Dallys

About Dallys-Tom Medali

Dallys lives in New York City. He is a Certified Public Accountant and Certified Fraud Examiner. He works primarily with the Banking Industry on some high profile Compliance and Consulting assignments. Dallys started writing at a young age in French, his native language and won many awards for his French poetry. "Coming Back" is his first Collection of poems written and published in English.

Other Books by this Author

Le Manuel du Milliardaire
Guide pratique, 2010
Editions Solara (USA) - ISBN 978-1-947838-00-0
Smashwords (USA) – ISBN 9781458105950

Légendes Inédites d'Afrique
Contes, 2010,
Editions Solara (USA) - ISBN 978-1-947838-02-4
Smashwords (USA) - ISBN 9781458198273

Belles Poésies de Cœur et de Corps
Poèmes, 2009
Editions Solara (USA) - ISBN 978-1-947838-01-7
Editions Dédicaces (Canada) - ISBN 9781926723372

Perles et Pensées
Poèmes, 2010
Editions Solara (USA) - ISBN 978-1-947838-03-1
Smashwords (USA) - ISBN 9781458099174

L'Evangile Pratique
Synthèse, 2015
Editions Solara (USA) - ISBN 978-1-947838-05-5
Smashwords (USA) - ISBN 9781310529061

La Bible Essentielle
Synthèse, 2017
Editions Solara (USA) - ISBN 978-1-947838-06-2

EBooks: http://www.smashwords.com/profile/view/dallystom
Paperback: http://www.lulu.com/spotlight/medali
Author Page: http://www.dallystom.com/books
Email: dallystom@gmail.com

www.ingramcontent.com/pod-product-compliance
Lightning Source LLC
Chambersburg PA
CBHW021348090426
42742CB00008B/777